THE STORY OF
YOUR MOUTH

THE STORY OF
YOUR MOUTH

*by Dr. Alvin Silverstein
and Virginia B. Silverstein*

illustrated by
Greg Wenzel

Coward-McCann, Inc.   New York

Library of Congress Cataloging in Publication Data
Silverstein, Alvin.
  The story of your mouth.
  Includes index.
  Summary: Discusses the many different functions of the
mouth and describes the physical characteristics and
duties of the individual structures it contains.
  1. Mouth—Juvenile literature. [1. Mouth]
I. Silverstein, Virginia B. II. Title.
QP146.S54 1983   612′.31   82-14234
ISBN 0-698-30742-9

CONTENTS

Gateway to the Body

One thing guaranteed to upset a new mother is her baby's habit of putting everything into its mouth. When the mother gets more experienced, she realizes that the baby isn't trying to be naughty. This is just one way of finding out about the world. The shape and feel and taste of things are just as interesting to a young child as their colors and sounds. The mouth is a sensitive part of the body's information-gathering system.

As we get older, the sense messages we receive through the mouth become less important to us—except when we are hungry. But the mouth itself is still a vital part. It is the chamber through which food and drink enter the body. It is also the organ that shapes the sounds by which we communicate with others. In addition, it is an opening through which we sometimes breathe.

The mouth is a very varied chamber. It contains a number of structures adapted to getting food and breaking it down into nourishing bits. Some of the mouth

structures do double or even triple duty, as sense organs
and as organs of speech. You probably have a fairly good
idea already of what parts your mouth contains. But you
may not know as much about what makes up the mouth
structures and what they do. Let's find out more about
the story of your mouth.

8

1 The Inside Story

"You are what you eat." There is a great deal of truth in this saying. The foods we eat give us the building materials that our bodies need in order to grow. It is true in another way too. An animal's body (especially its mouth) is well designed for the kind of food it eats.

Blood-sucking animals have a very simple mouth, super streamlined for the simple way that they feed. A mosquito, for example, has a mouth part that is called a *proboscis* and is shaped like an injection needle. The proboscis pierces the skin of a person or animal and sucks up blood just as you would drink a soda through a straw.

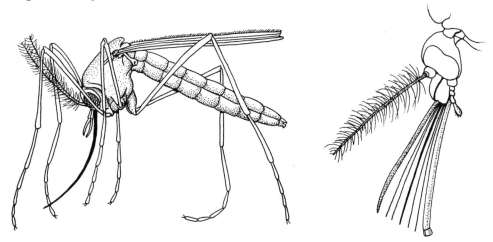

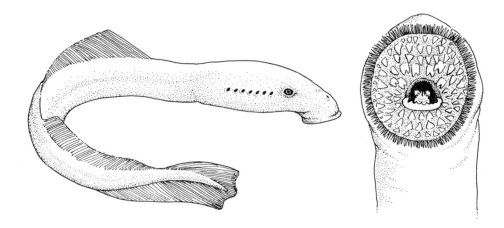

A fish called a lamprey has a mouth like a suction cup. It clamps onto the body of another fish and sticks tight. Its tongue is like a tiny saw that cuts a hole through the other fish's skin. Then the lamprey sucks a meal of blood while it tags along for a free ride.

People too can get along on a liquid diet if they have to. But like most animals, we prefer a lot of different kinds of food. We have a much more complicated mouth than mosquitoes or lampreys, and it lets us enjoy chewy steaks and crunchy nuts, as well as fruits, vegetables and juices.

The entrance to the mouth is guarded by a pair of fleshy *lips*. When they are closed, they seal the mouth tightly. The lips are much redder than the skin of the face around them, because they have a rich blood supply. The blood is carried by many tiny branching blood vessels, lying close to the surface. The red color of the blood shows through the thin, delicate covering of the lips. This covering lacks the horny substance that helps to make skin tough and durable. So, the lips may crack easily unless they are moistened often. A protective cream may help to keep them smooth and healthy.

The lips are one of the most sensitive parts of the body. Tiny nerve cells send messages racing to the brain when something touches them. Few other areas of the body have as many of these sensory nerves. (That is why kissing feels so nice.) The lips can also pick up small

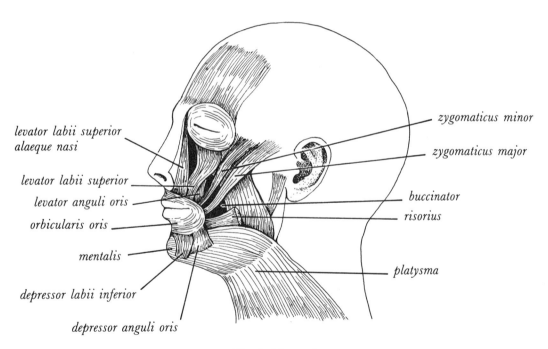

levator labii superior alaeque nasi

levator labii superior

levator anguli oris

orbicularis oris

mentalis

depressor labii inferior

depressor anguli oris

zygomaticus minor

zygomaticus major

buccinator

risorius

platysma

The facial muscles.

changes in temperature. (Does your mother feel your forehead with her lips when she wants to know if you have a fever?) Being sensitive to touch and pressure, heat and cold is a very useful ability for the gateway to the mouth. You use this ability when you bring a spoonful of soup to your lips to see whether it is cool enough to drink.

For most animals, the lips are simply a part of the body's eating system. Giraffes, for example, use their lips to pull the tender leaves off tree branches. But for people, lips are important in another way, too. They are a part of the way we communicate with each other. A smile, a frown, an angry snarl—in each case the lips give a clue to how we feel, and it can be read without a single spoken word. Lips also help to form the sounds of speech, shaping the vowel sounds and working by themselves or together with the teeth to make consonant sounds like *b, f, m, p,* or *r.*

The lips can move so freely and in so many varied ways through the action of a complex set of muscles. The lips themselves are mostly made of muscle, and they are attached to other muscles of the jaws and cheeks. There is a large muscle formed into a circular ring that runs all the way around the mouth. When this muscle contracts, the lips purse up into a kiss. There are also special muscles that can raise the corners of the lips into a smile or pull them down into a frown. The lips are opened and closed by the heavy jaw muscles, which also work in chewing.

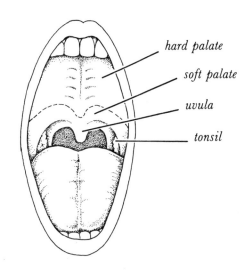

hard palate

soft palate

uvula

tonsil

(Only the lower jaw can move; the upper jaw is solidly built into the skull bones.)

The lips open into a chamber called the *mouth cavity.* This chamber has a curving roof called the *palate.* If you run your tongue over the roof of your mouth, you will find that it is very hard in the front part. Toward the back, where it is more difficult to feel with your tongue, the roof of the mouth is much softer. The front part is called the *hard palate.* It is made of bone.

Actually, the hard palate starts out as two halves. But very early—before a baby is born—the two halves of the hard palate join together to form a solid roof for the mouth. Sometimes the two halves of the palate fail to join. Then the child is born with a condition called *cleft palate:* there is a hole in the roof of the mouth. There may also be a cleft in the upper lip. That condition is called a *harelip.* (Hares and rabbits have a natural cleft in their upper lip, which helps them to pull in the tender shoots of plants that they eat.) Cleft palate and harelip can be repaired rather easily now by surgery.

The *soft palate* toward the back of the mouth cavity is not made of bone. It is made of strong muscles, which help in swallowing. It ends in a dangling flap called the

13

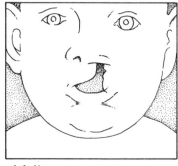

cleft lip

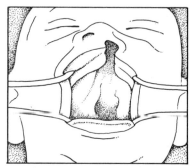
cleft lip and palate

uvula. If you look in the mirror and say "Ah-h-h," you will be able to see the U-shaped uvula hanging down. When you swallow, the soft palate is drawn upward. It acts as a trap door, closing off the passage leading up toward the nose. If you try to talk or laugh while drinking, the trap door may not close properly. Then liquid backs up into your nose, and you must cough and sputter until it is out.

The floor of the mouth cavity is formed by the lower jawbone. This bone, called the *mandible,* is the movable part of the jaw. It is shaped like a horseshoe, and it branches upward at each end to connect with the skull bones. A little knob at the end of each branch fits neatly into a round hollow in the skull bones. (If a person yawns too widely, the ends of the mandible may slip out of their sockets, very painfully dislocating the jaw.) Although the upper jaw is part of the skull and cannot move at all, the lower jaw can move in several ways. It can flap up and

14

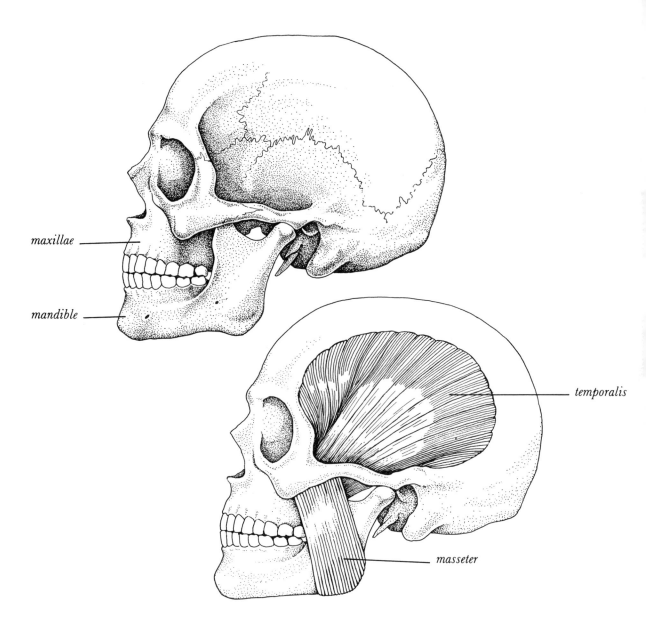

maxillae

mandible

temporalis

masseter

The jawbones form the bony framework of the mouth cavity. Only the lower jaw (the mandible) can move. The upper jaw (the maxillae) is solidly attached to the other bones of the skull. Heavy straplike muscles attached to the jaws and skull help in chewing.

down, move forward and back, and move from side to side. All these movements are useful in chewing, and also in speaking.

The jaw is moved by some very powerful muscles. They can clamp the jaws together with a force of 200

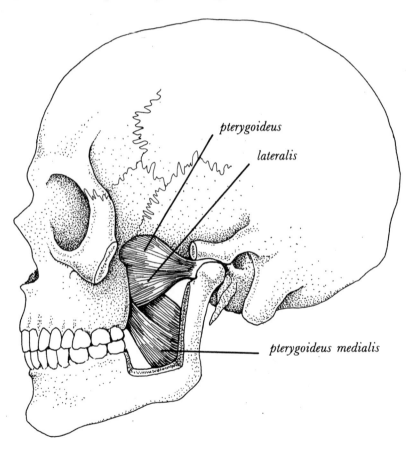

pterygoideus

lateralis

pterygoideus medialis

Attachment of jaw muscles

pounds. Circus performers on the high wire or trapeze sometimes use these muscles in an exciting act; gripping a small bar in their teeth, they dangle high in the air, holding up the entire weight of the body with just their jaw muscles.

The muscles of the jaws and cheeks form the side walls of the mouth cavity. The rear of the cavity leads into a tube called the *pharynx*. (That is the technical name for what you think of as the throat.) The pharynx is a double-duty passageway. It carries air from the nose down toward the lungs. It also carries food and liquids down toward the stomach.

A little below the opening from the mouth, the pharynx branches into two tubes: the air pipe, or *trachea*, and the food pipe, or *esophagus*. When you swallow, a leaf-shaped trap door called the *epiglottis* closes the opening to the trachea, so that no liquid or food particles will go down the air pipe. Sometimes, especially if you are eating too fast, the epiglottis fails to close. Then you swallow something "down the wrong pipe" and must cough it up again. Gobbling food or talking while you eat may also cause the opposite problem—swallowing air down the esophagus. The swallowed air can make you feel very uncomfortable until you burp it up. (In some parts of the world, it is considered good manners to burp loudly after a meal. That is the way you show the host or hostess how much you enjoyed the food.)

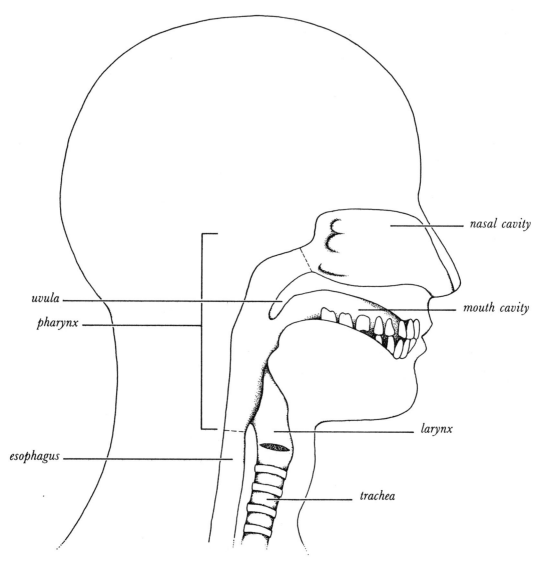

nasal cavity

uvula

pharynx

mouth cavity

larynx

esophagus

trachea

The nasal and mouth cavities open into the pharynx, which leads down into the airpipe (trachea) and food pipe (esophagus).

People normally breathe through their noses. But since the mouth cavity is also connected to the air pipe, through the pharynx, mouth breathing is also possible. You are probably very glad of this when you have a cold and your nose is stuffed up.

In emergencies, mouth breathing may even be a life saver. When people are caught in a fire or are drowning in water, they may stop breathing. They seem to be dead. But if they are rescued in time, they may be revived by mouth-to-mouth resuscitation. The rescuer breathes directly into the victim's mouth, forcing air from his or her own lungs down into the victim's lungs. The cells of the body, especially those of the brain, cannot live long without oxygen from the air. By breathing into the victim's mouth, the rescuer provides the precious oxygen until the victim's own breathing starts up again.

Occasional mouth breathing may be very useful, but some people get into the habit of breathing through their mouths all the time; and that is not a very good thing. Either the nose or the mouth can serve as a passageway for air entering the body. But the nose is better designed to be the gateway to the air passages. It is not just a passageway, but also a combination filter and heater. Bristly hairs at the entrance to the nose screen out large particles, and the slimy mucus in the nasal lining traps smaller ones. Air passing through the nose is warmed and moistened as it flows through the maze of the nasal passageway. Air breathed in through the mouth doesn't get any of this special treatment. It just goes straight into the pharynx. It is cold, dry, and sometimes dirty. Mouth breathing tends to dry out the lining of the mouth and throat and make a person's throat feel sore.

The inside of the mouth cavity is lined with soft, delicate tissue. It is something like skin, but it does not have the horny protective substance that skin has. The mouth lining is even thinner and more delicate than the covering of the lips, and it must constantly be kept moist. Its rich blood supply gives it a pink color.

Three pairs of glands pour fluids into the mouth cavity through tiny tubes or ducts. They are called *salivary glands,* and the fluid they produce is called *saliva.* This fluid forms a smooth, slippery lubrication for the mouth lining. Saliva also starts the digestion of food, as we shall see in Chapter Four.

Just inside the lips and cheeks there is a set of shiny white *teeth.* One horseshoe-shaped row of teeth grows up from the lower jaw, while a matching row of teeth grows down from the upper jaw. We can see only a part of any tooth; the whole structure extends deep into the soft tissues of the gums and ends in roots that are anchored firmly on the jawbone. The gums form a collar around the base of each tooth; they help to support and protect the teeth. Healthy gums are firm and pink.

Although teeth can be used for things like snipping off

the end of a sewing thread or dangling from a bar on the high wire, their main job is chewing food. They break down solid foods into smaller pieces that can more easily be swallowed. The human set of teeth includes three main kinds: chisel-shaped teeth good for cutting; pointed teeth for tearing; and large, broad teeth that are good for crushing and grinding foods.

Rising out of the floor of the mouth cavity is the large, fleshy *tongue*. One of the tongue's jobs is to move food around, shape it into a soft ball-shaped mass for swallowing, and then give it a final shove back into the pharynx. The surface of the tongue contains tiny structures called *taste buds*. These are the tiny sense organs that permit us to appreciate the sweetness of honey, the salt on a pretzel, the sour tang of vinegar in salad dressing, the bitterness of some medicines, and all the other flavors of our foods and drinks. The tongue also works to form many of the consonant sounds of our speech, by pressing in various ways against the palate.

Teeth, tongue, and salivary glands are the main working parts of the mouth. Let's take a closer look at these structures and the jobs that they do.

2 Tooth Tales

With just a piece of a jawbone, *paleontologists*—scientists who study ancient bones or fossils—can often figure out a great deal about what an ancient animal looked like. In fact, a single tooth can tell them a lot about how the animal lived and what it ate.

Some animals eat only plants. We call these animals *herbivores*. They feed on plant leaves, roots, fruits or seeds. Many plant-eating animals have well-developed cutting teeth. Large, chisel-shaped teeth in the front of the mouth snip off leaves and stems or gnaw chunks of roots with ease. The beaver has such big, strong front teeth that it can even gnaw through the trunks of trees. Grazing animals like horses and cows are plant eaters, too. Their big, heavy back teeth are good for grinding up mouthfuls of leaves or grains.

Animals that hunt for a living are called *carnivores,* and they have a different set of teeth. Dogs, cats, and other meat eaters have long, pointed fangs. They use them to bite into their prey and tear the meat into pieces small enough to swallow. They have cutting and grinding teeth too, but those are not very well developed. (If you watch a pet cat or dog eating, you may notice that it does not chew its food very well. It just swallows it down in chunks.)

The teeth of some animals show clearly that they are plant eaters. Other animals' teeth are just right for eating meat. But human teeth tell a different story. The teeth in a human mouth are ready for anything. Our cutting teeth are not as well developed as those of a beaver, but they are good enough to take a bite out of an apple or a carrot. Our grinding teeth are not as big and broad as those of a horse, but they can crunch up nutmeats and can mash vegetables into a soft pulp. We don't have long fangs like a cat or a dog, but we can handle even a tough piece of steak well enough. We have a very good set of teeth for an *omnivore*—that is, an animal that eats everything.

The complete set of teeth in an adult totals thirty-two— sixteen teeth in the upper jaw and sixteen in the lower jaw. At the front of the mouth are eight *incisors*, or cutting teeth—four up and four below. Then come four pointed "eye teeth," or *canines,* one in each quarter of the jaw. "Canine" means doglike; the eye teeth are called canines because they are like the fangs of a dog. After the canines, there are eight *bicuspids,* two in each quarter of the jaw. Each of them has two pointed peaks, or "cusps." (Their name, "bicuspid," means "two-pointed.") The bicuspids are a sort of compromise: They can tear foods, but not quite as well as the canines; and they can crush and grind foods, but not quite as well as the teeth at the back of the jaws, the *molars.* The twelve molars that complete the human set of teeth (three in each corner of the jaw) are also called *tricuspids*, because they have "three points" on their chewing surface.

When the mouth is closed, the two rows of teeth, upper and lower, fit neatly together into a bite. Cusps on the lower teeth fit into hollows in the upper teeth, and vice versa. The teeth in the lower jaw are a little smaller than the upper teeth, so the whole row of lower teeth fits just inside the upper ones.

Deciduous teeth (baby teeth). Adult teeth.

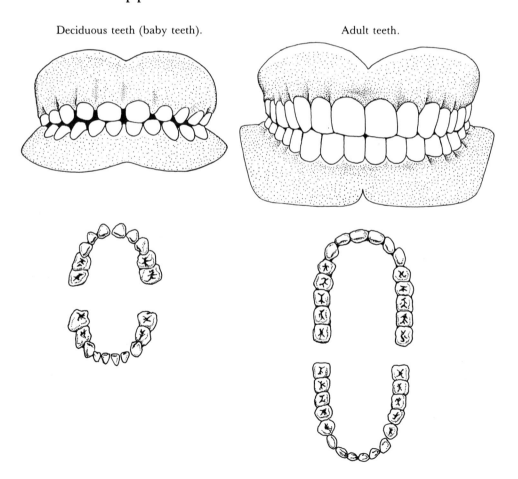

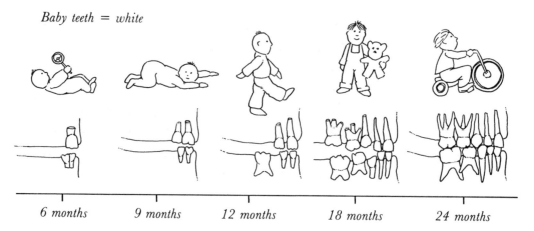

Baby teeth = white

6 months   9 months   12 months   18 months   24 months

The adult teeth are usually a person's second set. They are much too large (and there are too many of them) to have fit into the tiny jaw of a baby. Children have a somewhat different set of teeth, smaller ones, that number only twenty. They include eight incisors, four canines, and eight molars.

Babies are toothless when they are born. But although no teeth are showing, they are already formed, down in the baby's soft pink gums. The first teeth (the four front incisors) usually poke out of the gums when the baby is five to eight months old. The other four incisors follow soon after. The gums are usually a little swollen while the teeth are erupting, and the baby may be cranky when it is teething. The first four molars appear when the baby is about a year; and shortly after that, the canines slide neatly into the gaps between the incisors and molars. (It seems a little strange that the teeth don't erupt from the

26

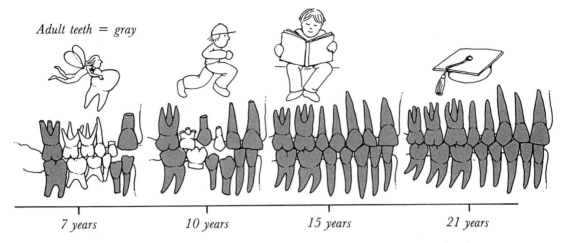

Adult teeth = gray

| 7 years | 10 years | 15 years | 21 years |

gums in order, but the first molars usually appear before the canines.) Finally, when the baby is about two years old, the last four molars of the baby teeth erupt. These ages are just averages, of course. A child can get teeth sooner or later than the average times and still be perfectly normal.

At around six years old, two important events occur in the life of the teeth. The first permanent molars, the "six-year molars," break through the gums just behind the baby molars, and the first of the baby teeth (the front incisors) start to fall out. The next few years are a very active time for the "tooth fairy." (A recent survey at Northwestern University School of Dentistry showed that inflation has hit the tooth fairy just as hard as everything else these days. A baby tooth left under a child's pillow is now bringing an average of 66 cents; fifteen years ago, the average was only 30 cents.)

Usually the baby teeth fall out in the order in which they came in. They are replaced by larger permanent teeth that have formed in the gums underneath them. First the baby incisors are replaced by permanent incisors. The baby canines are replaced by larger, permanent canines. (This may happen after the first baby molars fall out.) But the baby molars are not replaced by molars; the teeth that erupt in place of them are bicuspids.

By the time a child is twelve or thirteen, usually the baby teeth have all been replaced, and a second set of permanent molars is coming in behind the first ones. The last set of molars won't appear until the age of seventeen or older. These third molars are called "wisdom teeth," probably because they appear when a person is just about grown up and supposedly "wise."

Many people never get any wisdom teeth. The last molars may not form at all, or they may stay in the gums, firmly wedged against the teeth next to them. Even when the wisdom teeth erupt normally, they may tend to decay and then have to be extracted. Scientists say it is just as well that wisdom teeth seem to be disappearing. People today do not eat as rough a diet as their ancestors thousands of years ago. We don't eat as many whole grains and raw foods, and the soft cooked foods in our diet don't give our jaws as much exercise. We can get along very nicely with only twenty-eight teeth. Modern people's jaws seem to be getting a little smaller than those of our long-ago ancestors. Perhaps some time in the future, no one will have wisdom teeth any more.

Some animals, such as sharks, keep on growing new teeth all their lives. When a shark's front teeth get worn down, they fall out. Then the other teeth move forward to fill up the space, and new teeth grow in at the back. Unfortunately for us humans, two sets of teeth are all we ever get. If any of the permanent teeth are lost, there will be no new ones to replace them.

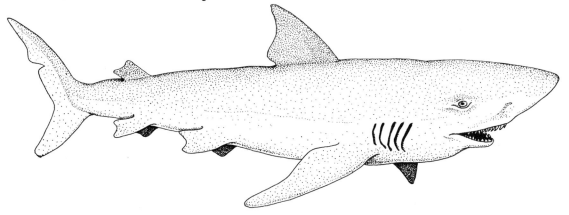

A shark's teeth are just simple pointed cones, which grow out of the skin of its mouth. Human teeth are much more complicated. Each tooth has three main parts. The part that sticks out of the gums is called the *crown*. Just below the gum line is the *neck* of the tooth. The third part, the *root*, grows deep into the gum and fits into a socket on the jawbone. The roots of teeth anchor them securely, so that they don't wobble even when you are

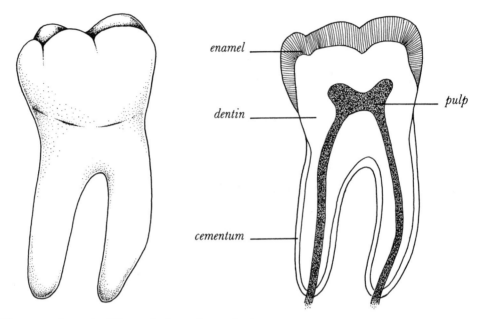

enamel

dentin

cementum

pulp

The parts of a tooth. (The tooth shown is a molar.)

chomping down on a nut or a carrot stick. (Chewing pressures can run as high as thirty thousand pounds per square inch.)

Chewing food in three meals a day (plus snacks) through a whole lifetime is hard work—so hard that you might wonder why the teeth don't eventually wear away. Actually, teeth do wear down a little as the years go by, but not very much. Their crowns are covered with *enamel*, the hardest substance in the body. Inside the enamel layer, the body of the tooth is made of a bonelike substance called *dentin*. Both enamel and dentin are mostly made up of calcium salts, but enamel is harder and denser than dentin. In the center of the tooth there is a hollow channel filled with soft tissue, blood vessels and nerves. This is the *pulp*. The nerves inside the pulp of a tooth can carry pain messages to the brain. A toothache is a warning signal that something bad is happening to a tooth. For example, if you get hit in the mouth with a baseball, your teeth are moved forcefully, and they may be sore for days afterward. If decay has eaten a hole all the way through the enamel and dentin to the pulp, the nerves in the tooth will complain, very painfully, about it.

Probably you have been told many times that if you don't brush your teeth regularly, or if you eat too much sugary food, you will get tooth decay. What is tooth decay? What is so bad about eating sugary foods? How does tooth brushing help? And are some toothpastes really better than others?

Scientists have done a great deal of research on *dental caries,* or tooth decay. They have found that it starts with a deposit called *plaque,* which builds up on teeth when they are not cleaned regularly and thoroughly. Plaque is a mixture of bits of leftover food, worn-out cells shed by the covering of the gums, and bacteria. The bacteria feed on the bits of food (sugar is an especially good food for them), grow and multiply. As they grow, they produce an acid, and the acid slowly eats holes through the tooth enamel.

Animals that are raised in special germ-free cages and never come in contact with bacteria throughout their whole lives, never get tooth decay, even if they eat a diet full of sugars. But we are not germ-free. Our skin and our mouths swarm with bacteria. Most of these microbes are harmless. But some of them can cause tooth decay if they get a chance. If you don't brush your teeth regularly, and if you feed the bacteria plenty of nourishing sugars, you will be giving them a chance to eat holes in your teeth.

What about toothpastes? Anton van Leeuwenhoek, a seventeenth-century Dutch lens maker, was the first man ever to see bacteria. He found them in scrapings from his own teeth, even though he brushed them every day with a paste of salt and water and picked out food particles from between them with a toothpick. When your grandparents were young, there were quite a few brands of toothpaste and tooth powder available. But there wasn't much difference between them—except that some were so hard and gritty that they could scour the enamel right off the teeth. None of them was really much better at protecting teeth than Leeuwenhoek's salt, or than baking soda, another homemade tooth powder. (They did taste better, though.)

But then scientists discovered a new toothpaste ingredient that did help stop tooth decay. They noticed that people who lived in places where there were large amounts of fluoride salts in the water had much fewer cavities in their teeth than most other people. First one toothpaste manufacturer and then others started adding fluoride to toothpaste, hoping that it would cut down tooth decay. It worked.

Dentists can also apply fluoride coatings directly to the teeth after a routine cleaning, and many communities add fluoride to their drinking-water supplies. There have been some very angry arguments about fluoridation. But so far there is no evidence that small amounts of fluorides hurt anybody, and there is plenty of evidence that it makes teeth more resistant to decay. The fluoride combines chemically with salts in the tooth enamel and makes the coating tougher.

A recent survey of nearly 40,000 schoolchildren, sponsored by the National Institute of Dental Research, showed that the number of cavities in children's teeth has dropped by nearly one third in the last ten years. What's more, the number of children who have no cavities at all is going up. The use of fluorides in drinking water and toothpastes is probably one reason for the drop in tooth decay. Another may be that people are learning better eating habits and better tooth care. Some dentists are using special sealants, protective coatings, that are applied to the teeth and last for seven years or more. Dental researchers are also testing a new vaccine to protect people against tooth-decay bacteria. It is in a drinkable form, like the oral polio vaccine that protects people against the polio virus.

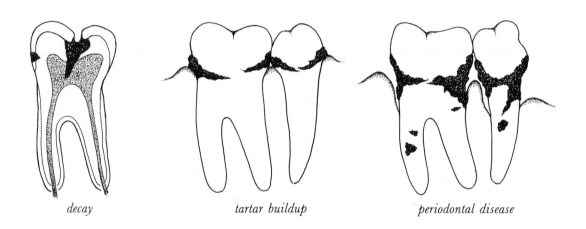

decay   *tartar buildup*   *periodontal disease*

Good tooth care includes more than just regular brushing. Brushing removes plaque from the tooth surfaces, and it gives the gums some healthy stimulation. But it doesn't do much about food particles caught between the teeth. The use of dental floss can help to remove plaque from places that the toothbrush can't reach. Cleaning down around the gum line is especially important. Plaque can build up there and harden into rocklike *tartar*. The tartar deposits may irritate the gums and make them sore and inflamed. Then the gums may shrink away, and the cementlike substance anchoring the tooth roots on the jawbone may dissolve, leaving the teeth loose and wobbly. This unpleasant condition is called *pyorrhea,* or *periodontal disease.* ("Pyorrhea" refers to the pus that is formed, and "periodontal" literally means "around the teeth.") If it gets bad enough, the teeth may even fall out.

When cavities do form in teeth, the dentist can fill them with metal or plastic compounds. First the area of decay must be thoroughly cleaned out, so that there will be no bacteria left to form a new cavity under the filling. That is what the dentist's drilling is all about.

Many people are afraid to go to the dentist, because they expect the treatments to hurt. But dental work is much less painful than it used to be. High-speed drills work cleaner and faster, and they are cooled with a stream of water or air, so that they do not build up heat. An injection of Novocaine into the gums blocks the messages from the pain nerves, so that you do not feel the dentist working on your teeth. Sometimes the dental patient breathes in a pain-killer in the form of a gas, or receives an injection to put him or her to sleep while the work is being done. Nitrous oxide, one of the drugs used in this way, is sometimes called "laughing gas" because it may make people feel happy and giggly. Usually a gas or injection to put the person to sleep is used for a very large job, or when the dentist is removing a badly decayed tooth. When a tooth is removed, it can be replaced by a false tooth.

Sometimes, when a tooth is so badly decayed that the infection has reached the inner pulp cavity, it can still be saved by a technique called root-canal therapy. The dentist kills and removes the nerve, replacing it with a firm plug. The tooth will then be dead, but it can still work in chewing.

Dentists today are using various new techniques to save and repair teeth. Some new plastics can be used to cover over flaws in teeth and even to rebuild broken teeth. They bind tightly to the natural tooth substance and can be tinted to blend in perfectly.

In a normal mouth, the teeth are evenly spaced and come together comfortably in a bite. But not everybody has a normal mouth. Sometimes the jaw is too small for a full set of teeth, and they are crowded, with some of them crooked and out of line. (This happens most often in the lower jaw.) Sometimes the upper front teeth stick out ("buck teeth"), so that there is a big gap between the upper and lower front teeth when the mouth is closed. (A little gap is normal, but a large one may make it difficult to bite and chew effectively.) More rarely, the lower jaw may stick out, so that the lower front teeth are in front of the upper ones. Some people have missing teeth—some of the teeth in the permanent set just never form. Others have too many teeth, which may stay inside the gums or may pop out in odd places, like the roof of the mouth.

The dental specialist who fixes bad bites is called an

orthodontist. Various combinations of wires, brackets and rubber bands exert a very slow, steady pressure on the teeth, so that they move into better positions in the mouth. The movement is very slow indeed, for it involves a rebuilding of the tooth sockets on the jawbone. Tiny bits of bone are dissolved away so that the tooth roots can move along the jawbone, and new bone is built up behind them to lock them firmly in place. Orthodontic treatment

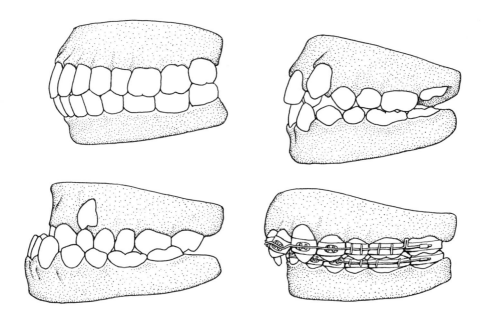

An orthodontist fixes various kinds of bad bites by moving teeth with combinations of wires and bands. A normal bite is shown in the upper left.

can take two years or more. This process may be short-
ened by a new technique now being developed. Instead
of the bulky braces that are worn all the time, researchers
at the University of Pennsylvania are using a small electri-
cal device, about the size of a dime. It is placed in the
mouth at bedtime, and while the person sleeps, tiny wires
resting against the gum send out an electric current that
stimulates the teeth to move in their bony sockets. The
researchers think similar devices may help stimulate
growth of the jawbone to make dentures fit better in
people who wear false teeth. They may help people with
periodontal disease. And they may even be used on
babies with cleft palate to make the bones of the roof of
the mouth grow together.

3 That Versatile Tongue

"Don't eat too many sweets. They're not good for you."
You have probably been hearing things like that for most
of your life. And they are true. Too much sugary food
not only can lead to tooth decay, but also can make people
overweight. Some doctors think that too much sugar in
the diet can even cause heart disease. And yet, you
probably like sweet foods. There's no need to feel guilty
about it. All people find sweet tastes pleasant. A liking for
sweet tastes is built into our heredity. At the beginning of
life it is necessary for survival. A newborn baby eagerly
drinks the sweet-tasting milk of its mother. It is only later
in life that a "sweet tooth" can get us into trouble. Fortunately, by that time we have learned to appreciate many
other tastes as well.

We perceive tastes with special sense organs called *taste
buds*. These are found on the upper surface of the
tongue. If you stick out your tongue and look at it in a
mirror, you will notice that it is not smooth. It has a

rough, pebbly texture. Under a high-power microscope, the little bumps on the surface of the tongue take on complicated shapes, like tiny flower buds or cabbage heads, surrounded by fingerlike projections. Inside the buds are nerve cells. They are sense nerves, but they do

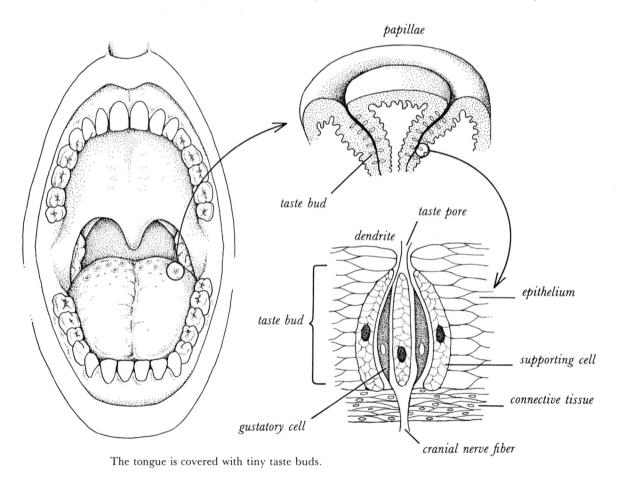

The tongue is covered with tiny taste buds.

not respond to heat or cold or touch. They are sensitive to chemicals.

There are four kinds of taste buds. Each kind responds to a particular taste—sweet, sour, salty and bitter. Taste buds are not found all over the tongue, but only in certain parts of it. Taste buds of the same kind are grouped together. Taste buds for sweet tastes are at the front of the tongue—the first part that dips into a mouthful of food or liquid. Taste buds for salt are at the sides toward the front, those for sour tastes farther back on the sides, and the taste buds for bitter tastes are spread across the back of the tongue.

It seems a little strange that there are only four kinds of taste buds when we can taste hundreds of different flavors. The flavors of most foods are blends of the four primary tastes, just as many different shades of color can be blended from the primary colors red, yellow and blue. Because the four kinds of taste buds are found on different parts of the tongue, sometimes we can taste two or more distinct flavors in the same food. For example, some medicines taste very sweet when they first enter the mouth, but bitter as they go down into the throat.

People generally find sweet tastes very pleasant and bitter tastes unpleasant. These reactions are part of the body's automatic warning system: sweet foods in reasonable amounts are usually wholesome, while many poisons have a bitter taste. Sour and salty tastes are pleasant in small amounts but unpleasant in large amounts. Researchers in Jerusalem found that sour and bitter tastes make the heart speed up 20 percent. The body reacts as though these tastes are a warning of danger.

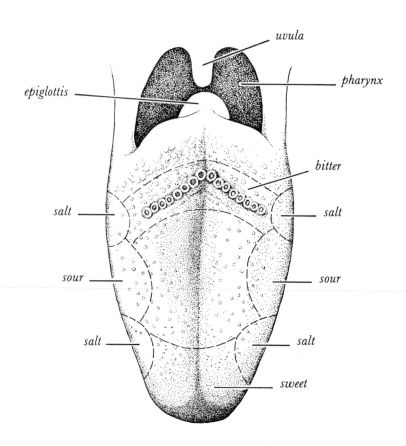

Distribution of taste buds on the tongue.

Another group of researchers found that tasty foods increase the appetite. Each new taste produces a new increase in appetite. So, a varied, tasty diet makes people eat more. The researchers suggested that people trying to lose weight should eat a very dull diet of bad-tasting foods.

Here's a taste experiment you can try yourself. Wipe your tongue very dry with a clean cloth, and then have someone sprinkle some crystals of sugar or salt on it. You will find that you can't tell whether it is sugar or salt. In fact, you can't taste anything. The taste sense works only when chemicals in a liquid solution come in contact with the taste buds, something we will discuss in the next chapter. Dry solids do not produce any taste sensations.

There is another odd thing about the taste sense. Have you noticed that when you have a cold and your nose is stopped up, foods don't have as much taste as usual? The reason is that what we think of as taste is partly our sense of smell. When the nose is blocked, we have to rely on just the taste buds on the tongue.

Adults have a total of about ten thousand taste buds. But with age, some of them break down. People find they can't taste things as sharply as they used to. Sometimes people suffer from a different taste complaint: things begin to taste peculiar, not the way they should. Favorite foods may suddenly begin to taste unpleasant. A lack of the mineral zinc in the diet may be the cause of this problem, and a zinc supplement can often clear it up dramatically.

Have you ever wondered why some people like certain foods very much, while others hate the same foods? Eggs, liver and spinach are examples of foods that produce very different reactions. Studies have shown that there are differences in the way people taste, and these differences are hereditary. There is a chemical called *phenylhydrazine* that tastes bitter to some people and sweet to others, while still others say they can't taste anything at all. A chemical called *phenylthiocarbamide* (PTC) is often used to test taste heredity. Most people find it bitter tasting, but between 15 and 30 percent of the population cannot taste PTC.

Other things too affect the way we react to tastes. Both people and animals tend to seek out foods that meet the body's needs. If they are lacking sugar, then they want to eat sweet-tasting foods. In the summer, when you sweat a lot and lose salt, you may find yourself craving salty foods. In one experiment, a group of babies old enough to eat with their fingers were given dishes of various foods and allowed to eat whatever they wanted. Sometimes the babies ate little bits of a number of foods and sometimes they gobbled down one food and left all the rest. But when the researchers checked the eating records over a period of several days they found that the babies were eating a fairly well-balanced diet.

Some of our reactions to food tastes are learned. A person (or an animal) who gets sick immediately after eating a particular food will often develop a dislike of that food taste and will avoid it in the future. This kind of learned taste reaction helps to protect us from eating things that are harmful.

Taste buds are not the only sense receptors on the tongue. There are also receptors for heat, cold and touch. The tongue is one of the most sensitive parts of the whole body. In one test of touch sensitivity, for example, two pointed rods are touched to the skin and slowly moved toward each other. At some distance, the person can no longer feel two distinct points—the touch seems to merge into one. On the skin of the back, two separate touches cannot be distinguished when they are closer than two inches. But on the tongue, two points can be felt separately when they are only $1/25$ inch apart.

Touch sensitivity is a useful characteristic for the tongue as it sweeps up food particles and shapes them into a ball-shaped mass for swallowing. The tongue is very agile. It can move up and down, in and out, hump up in the middle, and roll into a tube. (Some people can roll the tongue, but others can't, no matter how hard they try. Tongue rolling is a hereditary ability.) The tongue is almost solid muscle. Muscle fibers run up and down, across, and along the length of it. In addition to these internal muscles, the agile movements of the tongue are

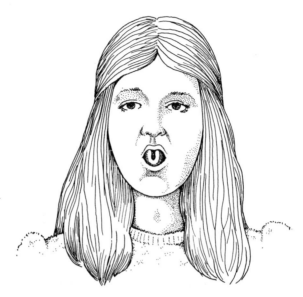

also controlled by straps of muscle that anchor it to the floor of the mouth and to the bones at the sides of the skull.

On the underside of the tongue, a fold of tissue running down the middle ties it down to the floor of the mouth. Sometimes this tissue, called the *frenulum,* runs the entire length of the tongue and keeps it from moving freely. When a baby is born "tongue-tied" in this way, the doctor usually cuts part of the frenulum to free the tongue, so that the baby will be able to talk properly.

The tongue plays a very important part in speech. If you doubt that, hold your tongue down with a finger and try to talk.

The sound of speech starts with a breath. Air from the lungs passes out through the *trachea,* or air pipe. Just

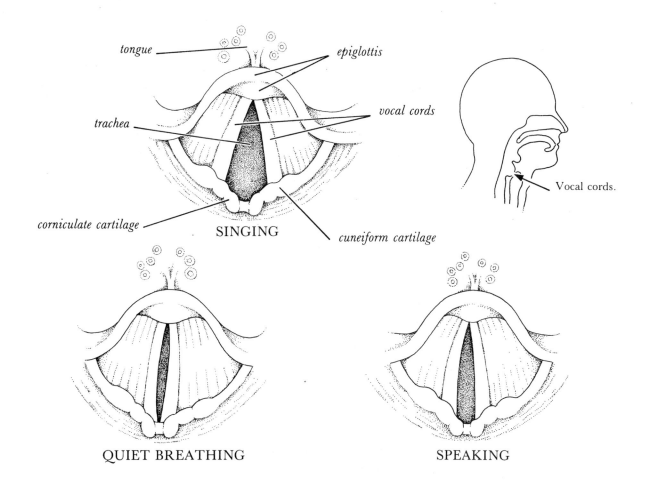

tongue

epiglottis

trachea

vocal cords

corniculate cartilage

SINGING

cuneiform cartilage

Vocal cords.

QUIET BREATHING

SPEAKING

before it reaches the *pharynx,* or throat, it flows through the voice box, or *larynx.* Stretched across the larynx are two folds of tissue, the *vocal cords.* When they are relaxed, the vocal cords leave a wide gap, through which air can flow freely. Breathing is silent when the vocal cords are relaxed. But if you want to talk, or sing, or make some other sound, you tighten the vocal cords. They narrow the gap, and the breaths passing through set the vocal cords vibrating like a plucked violin string. The vibration makes a sound. The *pitch* of the sound—how high or low it is—depends on how tight the vocal cords are. The tighter the cords, the higher the sound. (The length of the vocal cords also helps to determine the pitch. Women usually have a smaller larynx than men, and women's voices are usually higher-pitched than men's. Children, with their small larynxes, also have high voices that get lower as their bodies grow.)

The larynx produces voice sounds, but by itself it can't make speech sounds. If you open your mouth and make a sound while carefully keeping your tongue still, all you can produce is a long "Ah-h-h-h." Movements of the tongue, teeth and lips break up the flow of air from the larynx and help to change the sounds. The shape of the lips forms many speech sounds, and the teeth take part in some. (For example, the hissing *s* sound comes from forcing air out through almost closed teeth.) But the tongue takes part in forming even more of the speech sounds than the lips. Ventriloquists learn to speak fairly clearly while hardly moving their lips at all. But no one can speak clearly without a tongue.

4 Digestion Starts in the Mouth

A juicy steak is sizzling on the grill. The air is filled with its tempting aroma, and your mouth is already watering as you wait impatiently for it to be done. The steak hasn't been served yet, you haven't taken a single bite, and yet your body has already started on the first step in digesting it!

The watery fluid that fills your mouth is *saliva*. It is produced by three pairs of salivary glands.

The *parotid glands* are the largest salivary glands. They are found in the cheeks, just under and in front of each ear. They make a thin, watery fluid. It empties into the mouth cavity through small tubes (ducts) that open in the inner surface of the cheek, opposite the second molar of the upper jaw.

The *submaxillary glands* lie on the inner surface of the mandible (the lower jaw). The "maxilla" is the technical name for the upper jaw, so "submaxillary" actually means "below the upper jaw." The watery saliva of these glands empties into the mouth through ducts that open just behind the incisor of the lower jaw. It is important to brush and floss very thoroughly in this area, as well as around the second molar of the upper jaw, where the parotid saliva empties. Salts and other substances in the saliva contribute to the formation of *tartar*, which builds

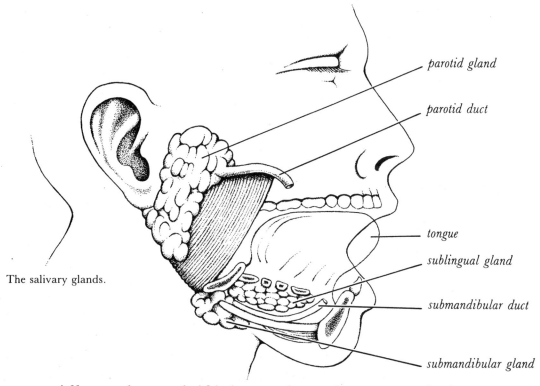

parotid gland

parotid duct

tongue

sublingual gland

submandibular duct

submandibular gland

The salivary glands.

up rapidly on the teeth if it is not cleaned away regularly.

The third pair of salivary glands is the *sublingual glands.* Their name means "below the tongue," because that is

51

where they are found—on the floor of the mouth. Their saliva empties into the mouth through a number of small ducts under the tongue. The saliva produced by the sublingual glands is thicker than that of the other two pairs. It has a rather slimy, sticky feel, very much like the mucus in the nose.

The three pairs of salivary glands pour more than a quart of saliva into the mouth each day. A certain amount is flowing all the time, keeping the mouth comfortably moist. When you are beginning a meal, the flow of saliva increases. Many things stimulate the flow. The taste (and even the smell) of food can start saliva flowing. The feel of food also plays a role; just holding a smooth pebble in your mouth can fool your salivary glands into pouring out their fluid. Looking at a picture of a delicious dessert in a magazine ad can start you salivating, and so can thinking about food when you are hungry.

The mind actually has a great effect on saliva production. More saliva flows when you are eating something you like than when you are eating something you dislike. Even when you are not eating (or thinking about eating), your mind and emotions affect the saliva flow. When you are calm and relaxed, your saliva is thin and plentiful. When you are frightened, angry or upset, smaller amounts of thicker saliva are produced, and your mouth may feel uncomfortably dry. A dry mouth may also be a sign that the body needs more water. The feeling of thirst prompts you to drink more fluids.

Even the thinnest saliva is not pure water. It contains a protein called *mucin,* which gives it its slippery feel, as well as various salts and enzymes. An *enzyme* is a protein that makes chemical reactions go. There are two main enzymes in saliva. *Ptyalin,* which is also called *salivary amylase,* is an enzyme that helps to digest foods. It breaks down starches into sugars. (If you chew on a cracker for a while without swallowing, you will find that it begins to taste sweet. Its starches are being broken down by the ptyalin in saliva.) The other salivary enzyme, *lysozyme,* splits apart chemicals on the outer coat of bacteria. It is a germ killer that helps to keep the mouth healthy.

The saliva that flows at the smell and taste of a "mouthwatering" steak actually does not digest the steak. Steak is made of mainly proteins and fats, and the salivary enzyme works only on starches. (It can help digest the potatoes you eat with the steak.) Even starches are not completely digested by the saliva in the mouth. It doesn't get a chance to act long enough. Just as it is starting to work on the foods, you swallow the mouthful. The the food is propelled down the esophagus into the stomach, where it is plunged into an acid bath that stops the action of ptyalin.

The saliva isn't wasted, though, for it does other helpful things. First of all, it provides the fluid that the taste buds need. (Remember that you can't taste foods in a completely dry mouth.) In addition, saliva helps to soften food particles and bind them together, so that they can be chewed and swallowed more easily.

"Slow down! Don't gobble your food! Chew thoroughly!" Has anybody every told you that? It is good advice, at least for people. Some animals can gobble their food down in chunks without chewing it. Seals do, for example. But in addition to the small fish and chunks of meat that a seal swallows whole, it also swallows stones that stay in its stomach and grind up the food it didn't

The Heimlich Maneuver
When someone is choking on a badly swallowed piece of food, pressing on their abdomen can force the food out and clear the airpipe.

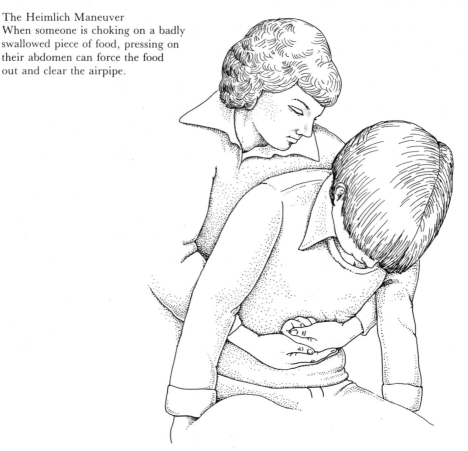

chew. Birds also swallow small stones to grind up the seeds they eat. We humans would find a stomach full of stones rather uncomfortable, though, so we must chew our food thoroughly before swallowing. The longer you chew, the more thoroughly the food will be mixed with saliva and the longer the salivary enzymes will have to work on the food. Soft, well-chewed food is also much easier to swallow. If you gulp down poorly chewed chunks of food, especially if you swallow them quickly or wash them down with a drink, they are more likely to "go down the wrong way." A badly swallowed chunk of food may lodge in the windpipe. People can even choke to death that way! So take your time when you eat, and chew thoroughly.

Let's see what happens to a bite of steak sandwich in the mouth. Your teeth clamp down on the sandwich while your lips hold it steady, and your incisors cut off a convenient-sized bite. Saliva has already been flowing into your mouth, and it mixes with the food particles as you start to chew. Your tongue is busy moving the food around, turning it and shifting it from side to side so that your teeth can tear and crush the food particles into smaller and smaller pieces. (The mechanical action of chewing is also referred to as *mastication*.) Meanwhile, ptyalin in the saliva is starting to break down the starches in the bread. This is the start of the chemical reactions of digestion.

After a while, when the mouthful feels right (or when you are too impatient to chew any longer), your tongue shapes the soft, soggy mass into a ball. This ball of chewed food is called a *bolus*. The tongue picks up the bolus and shoves it back toward the throat. You can decide consciously when you want to start swallowing. But once you have started, you can't stop. Automatic mechanisms take over, and the swallowing process is out of your control.

Swallowing starts when the tongue presses the bolus against the soft palate in the back of the mouth. Muscles lift the soft palate and close off the passage leading to the nose. Up to this point, you could still stop and spit out the food. But then the bolus is pushed into the pharynx. Now it's too late to change your mind. Without any conscious thought, your body goes into action in a complicated sequence that makes sure the food goes down your esophagus and nowhere else. The epiglottis at the top of the larynx folds down like a trap door to close off the air pipe, and the tongue shuts off the mouth cavity. The soft palate is already blocking the tube up to the nose. So the bolus has nowhere to go but down the esophagus.

Waves of muscle contraction in the walls of the esophagus help to send the food on its way. Gravity helps, too. (It's easier to eat sitting up than lying down.) Before the first astronauts went out into space, doctors worried about whether they would be able to eat in free fall, when there was no gravity to help them swallow their food. But

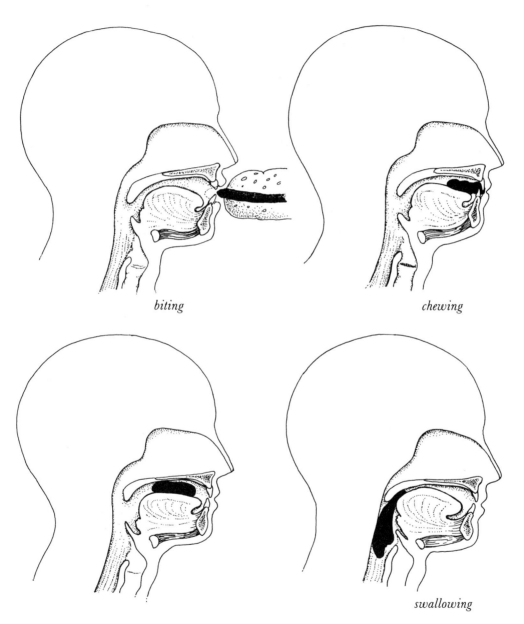

biting

chewing

swallowing

The tongue and teeth cooperate in preparing food for swallowing.

the astronauts didn't have any trouble eating; the esophagus can do the job without gravity, if necessary.

A ring-shaped muscle, or *sphincter,* at the top of the stomach opens to let the food in. Normally, when you are not eating, the stomach's spincter stays tightly closed. But sometimes it relaxes accidentally, and a bit of the stomach juices splashes up into the esophagus. (That is what causes the painful sensation of "heartburn.") Sometimes partly digested food may actually back up into the mouth. That happens often in babies, whose sphincters aren't very efficient yet, and they spit up mouthfuls of milk.

Down in the stomach, we've wandered quite a way from the story of your mouth. And yet, the story of digestion has barely begun. In the stomach, the two main themes of the mouth are repeated. Mechanical forces act on the food, mixing it and helping to break it down. (There aren't any teeth in the stomach; here the mechanical forces are powerful contractions of the stomach walls, which mix and churn the food.) Chemical forces, especially digestive enzymes, split the complicated chemicals of food into simpler chemicals. Much of the digestion of protein happens in the stomach.

After the stomach, food enters the long, looping tube of the small intestine. More enzymes act on the food substance, breaking down starches, proteins and fats into simple substances that can be taken into the body cells. As muscle contractions churn the food and move it along, nourishing substances pass into the blood. Eventually the undigested leftovers pass through the large intestine and out of the body.

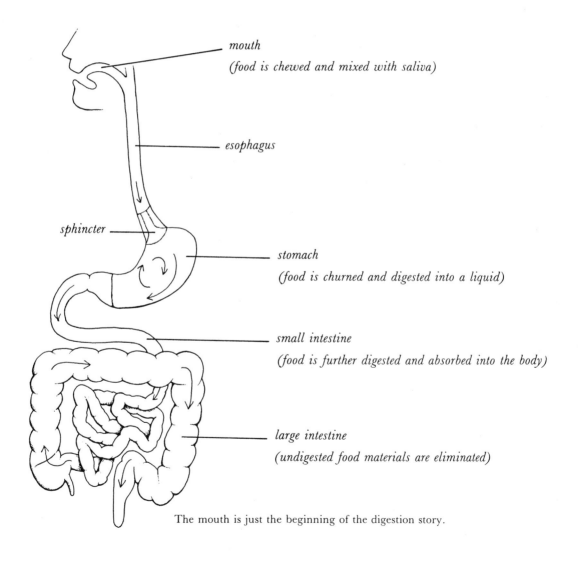

mouth
(food is chewed and mixed with saliva)

esophagus

sphincter

stomach
(food is churned and digested into a liquid)

small intestine
(food is further digested and absorbed into the body)

large intestine
(undigested food materials are eliminated)

The mouth is just the beginning of the digestion story.

5 When Things Go Wrong

A doctor who says "Stick out your tongue and say *Ah*" probably is not really interested in your tongue. To be sure, the tongue has some tales to tell about the health of the body. A furry whitish coating or unusual redness of the tongue may give clues to what is wrong. Scarlet-fever sufferers, for example, have a bright-red "strawberry tongue," along with a ring of whiteness around the mouth. But after a quick glance at your tongue, what the doctor really wants to peer at is your throat.

If you shine a flashlight into your mouth and look into it with a mirror, the first thing you see at the back of the mouth cavity is the *uvula*. That is the U-shaped flap of tissue that hangs down from the soft palate. Behind the uvula is the entrance to the pharynx, the throat cavity. The pharynx is not an empty tube. As you look through the opening, you can see two large rounded blobs of tissue, one at each side. These are the *tonsils*.

Normally the tonsils are a healthy pink color, like the

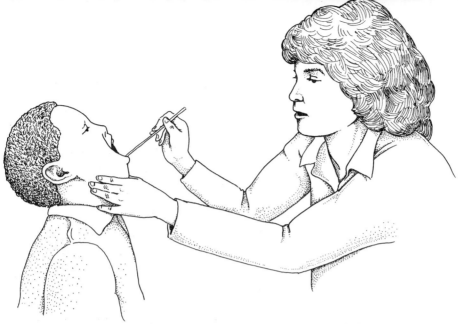

When a child has a sore throat, a throat culture can show whether it is a "strep throat" that might develop into rheumatic fever if it is not treated promptly.

rest of the throat. Although they are fairly large, they leave plenty of room for air and food to pass down the tube. But during colds and other illnesses, the tonsils get swollen and angry-looking. Instead of their shiny color, they may be bright red with patches of pus. They may swell up so much that they nearly close the pharynx.

Doctors used to think that if children had many attacks of *tonsillitis* (inflammation of the tonsils), with high fever and a lot of pain, the best thing to do was to take out the tonsils. *Tonsillectomy* was one of the commonest surgical operations.

Ideas have changed since then. Now most doctors believe that when the tonsils swell up with infections, they

61

are only doing their job. They are actually helping the body. For the tonsils are filled with special disease-fighting cells. They help to trap invading germs and filter them out before they can travel down to the lungs. So, nowadays, very few children have their tonsils taken out.

In addition to sore throats, the mouth cavity can suffer from various other problems. We have already talked about some problems of the teeth and gums. The general name for an inflammation of the gums is *gingivitis*. The gums may get red, puffy and sore. They may bleed easily when you brush your teeth. The most common reason is improper tooth care, which allows food particles to be trapped between the gums and teeth, and this causes tartar to build up on the teeth and rub against the gums. This may happen during orthodontic treatment, when the brackets of the braces make it hard to brush the teeth thoroughly.

Sometimes gingivitis is caused by a lack of enough Vitamin C in the diet. Sailors on long voyages used to get a disease called *scurvy*. One of the main symptoms was painful, bleeding gums. Finally a doctor figured out the reason. When sailors spent weeks or months away from port, they lived on a diet of salted meat and dry biscuits. They didn't eat any fresh fruits or vegetables that could supply Vitamin C. The doctor suggested that ships of the British navy should take supplies of limes with them. When they did, the sailors no longer came down with scurvy. This helpful idea gave Britishers their nickname of "Limeys."

Scurvy is rather rare now, but some mouth problems are still common. One of them is *canker sore*. You may suddenly notice a painful spot on the inside of your cheek or lips, or perhaps on the tongue or soft palate. If you look at the spot to see what is wrong, at first nothing may be showing. But after a day or two you can see a small punched-out hole in the mouth lining. A number of things can cause canker sores or make them worse. They may appear during a cold or an emotional upset. Anything that scratches the lining of the mouth may produce a sore—a toothbrush bristle, a bit of sharp nutmeat, or perhaps a rough spot on a tooth that rubs against the lining of the cheek.

Usually canker sores heal by themselves in ten to fourteen days. Soothing ointments or mouth rinses (even a warm salt solution) may give some comfort. An antibiotic called tetracycline can cut the healing time to five, six or seven days.

Cold sores or *fever blisters* are another common mouth problem. Actually, neither of the common names is a very good one. The sores sometimes appear during a cold or fever, but they are not caused by it. They are caused by infection with a virus called *herpes simplex* type 1. Until recently, doctors could not do much about cold sores, which are painful little blisters around the corners

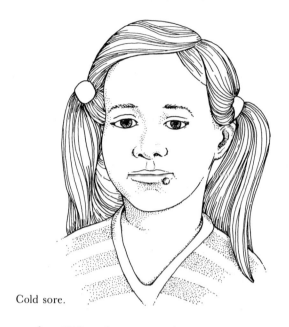

Cold sore.

of the mouth. (The herpes virus may also cause sores on the gums.) Some treatments, such as dabbing cold sores with ether, seem to make them heal faster, and ointments can help to soften the crusts and relieve the pain. In any case, the body itself can generally get cold sores under control in about two weeks. They heal up without leaving a scar.

Unfortunately, the body's defenses don't kill the herpes viruses. The cold sores disappear, but the virus stays in the body. It goes into hiding, in nerves around the mouth. Any stress, from a cold to an emotional upset, or even a sunburn, can make the cold sores pop out all over again. In the United States today, at least fifty million people suffer from attacks of cold sores at least once or twice a year.

Herpes infections are very contagious, especially when the sores are active. The person's saliva swarms with the viruses. They can be transferred to other people by kissing, by sharing a glass, and in any way that saliva comes in contact with a cut or sore. (Dentists often get herpes infections on their fingers from contact with their patients' saliva.)

Herpes infections are a nuisance, but cold sores usually are not very dangerous. There is one important exception. If you scratch a cold sore and then rub your eyes or handle contact lenses, you may develop a herpes infection in your eyes. The virus multiplies in the delicate eye tissues and may scar the cornea, the eye's transparent outer coat. Scars from herpes infections are the second-most-common cause of blindness in the United States.

Fortunately, researchers have recently developed new antiviral drugs that are effective agaisnt herpes viruses. Instead of making the virus go into hiding, the drugs can kill it. Researchers are also working on vaccines that may protect people from catching herpes infections.

One mouth problem that never killed anybody but has probably ruined a lot of friendships is *halitosis* or bad breath. Halitosis is very noticeable to other people, but the person who has it often has no idea that he or she has foul-smelling breath. The reason is that our smell sensors tend to "turn off" when they have been exposed to the same smell for a long time. We don't smell our own bad

breath, because we are used to it.

Antiseptic mouthwashes can help in cases of bad breath that is due to the buildup of decaying food particles and bacteria around the teeth. (Regular tooth brushing and flossing can help even more.) But sometimes the foul odor that seems to be coming from the mouth may actually be due to a problem down in the stomach or even the small intestine. Then mouthwashes won't help at all.

When you consider how many things go into the mouth—some of them dirty or even dangerous—it is surprising that this gateway to the body usually stays so healthy. Yet the mouth has many built-in defenses, from the bacteria-killing enzyme in saliva to very active processes of repair. Cuts and sores in the gums or mouth lining heal quickly, without leaving scars, and are soon replaced by healthy new tissue. Even the teeth, with a little help from modern dentistry and good, common-sense care, can last for a lifetime. For the most part, the story of your mouth is a success story—the tale of a well-engineered set of tools that work together tirelessly to do their jobs well.

Index